Emotion Relat

Identifying and Effectively Dealing with Narcissists, Sociopaths, Psychopaths and Toxic People

By Frank James

Table of Contents

Introduction

Emotional abuse (sometimes referred to as psychological abuse, verbal abuse, or chronic verbal aggression) is a form of non-physical abuse which tends to result in low self esteem, withdrawn or depressive behavior, increased anxiety, and even suicidal tendencies in the individual being abused.

Emotional abuse can take many forms and have many consequences. It differs from case to case and individual to individual. Some forms of emotional abuse include:

- Excessive yelling or swearing
- Insulting, name calling, or mocking
- Threatening or intimidating
- Ignoring or excluding
- Isolating
- Humiliating
- Denying abuse and/or blaming the victim

An important note here is that these things are not one time events but part of a pattern or cycle of behavior. Everyone loses their temper sometimes and starts yelling, swearing, or insulting people. However, when this happens regularly, it is likely symptomatic of a larger problem.

When your partner exhibits a pattern of such abusive behavior, he or she is likely a narcissist, sociopath, psychopath, or another type of toxic person. The abuse is typically followed by regret regarding the consequences of his or her actions and attempts to excuse the behavior either by blaming it on some external situation or blaming it on the victim of the abuse.

Examples of emotional abuse include the following behaviors:

- Threats of violence
- Intentionally causing fear (usually of abandonment)
- Lying

- Insulting or mocking (especially in front of others)
- Restricting your ability to socialize with others
- Making unreasonable demands

This list is by no means exhaustive. There are an endless number of ways that a person can emotionally abuse his or her partner. In most cases, the partner learns what you're most sensitive to or what your vulnerable points are and targets them in order to manipulate or control you.

Emotional abuse is a serious problem because it can cause many psychological problems. Some personal signs that you may be suffering from emotional abuse include:

- Feelings of isolation
- Rarely seeing friends and family
- Feelings of anxiety (especially in regard to your partner)
- Feelings of depression

- Low self-esteem and feeling inadequate or ineffectual
- Fearing for your own safety
- Feelings of excessive dependence on your partner

An Overview of Narcissists, Sociopaths, Psychopaths, and Toxic People

In many ways, the characteristics of these different types of people overlap. The emotionally abusive behavior is equally detrimental no matter what sort of person is doing it to you. However, there are some key differences which will be discussed in much greater detail in the following chapters. It is important to know what sort of person you are dealing with, not because it affects the consequences of the emotional abuse, but because you will be better able to deal with your specific situation if you know exactly what sort of problem you are dealing with.

In this chapter, you will just read a very brief overview about these different types. In the next chapters, you will get much more detail about them as well as advice for how to deal with each type of person.

The Narcissist

A narcissist is a person who is so absorbed in him or herself that he or she becomes incapable of caring or empathizing with others. This is different from a person who is simply selfish in that it causes severe problems in the narcissist's life. He or she is unable to form meaningful relationships and tends to push everyone away due to the disruptive narcissistic behaviors.

Narcissistic personality disorder is a diagnosable defect for which treatment options are available (albeit their efficacy varies highly). Within the broader category of narcissistic personality disorder are subtypes depending on the specific characteristics expressed by the individual. Those subtypes include unprincipled narcissist, amorous narcissist, compensatory narcissist, elitist narcissist, and fanatic narcissist. Each of these subtypes will be discussed in greater detail later on.

The Sociopath

A sociopath is one who suffers from antisocial personality disorder (alternatively known as dissocial personality disorder). Someone with this disorder exhibits a blatant disregard for (or conscious violation of) other's rights. A sociopath is characteristically deficient in morality and seems to lack a conscious.

They will typically have a criminal record or be plagued by legal problems. They are impulsive, aggressive and lack remorse. They differ from a narcissist in the sense that they are not necessarily self-absorbed. Furthermore, narcissists do not generally experience the same troubles with the law and are better able to distinguish right from wrong (or, at least know how others expect them to behave) since they, unlike a sociopath, ultimately are seeking the approval and admiration of others.

The Psychopath

A psychopath is very similar to a sociopath. He or she also lacks a sense of right or wrong and will often come into trouble with the law. In fact, within the psychiatric community, the precise distinction between the two is still argued. However, it is generally conceded that a psychopath is more dangerous than a sociopath.

Signs of psychopathology appear in early childhood (whereas sociopaths cannot be diagnosed until they are adults). It is believed that the causes of psychopathology ultimately lie in genetic and physical defects rather than specific social environments (as it is for antisocial personality disorder).

Furthermore, whereas a sociopath will typically direct his or her impulsivity or aggressive behavior toward those people around him or her (such as a partner, friend, or family member), a psychopath is indiscriminant and will treat all people with more or less equal disregard. If the person you are with is emotionally abusive to not only you but everyone else around, he or she is likely a psychopath.

The Toxic Person

A toxic person is not medically defined in psychiatry. Rather, this may be someone who does not suffer from any specific psychological or personality disorder but is still emotionally abusive anyway.

Alternatively, it may be someone who suffers from one of a number of other disorders which cause a person to be more likely to engage in emotional abuse. This introductory overview may sound vague now but this general category of toxic people will be discussed at length in chapter four.

So, if you do not feel at this point that any of the above three types fits the behavior of your partner, go on to chapter four to find out if any of the characteristics or descriptions there are more applicable. You should, of course, read through the other chapters as well to make sure you can safely rule them out. And, in any case, if you suspect a personality disorder of any kind, you should definitely consult a professional, trained psychiatrist or psychologist to help you identify exactly what you are dealing with.

Chapter 1: Abusive Relationships with Narcissists

In this chapter, you will learn more about the different subtypes of narcissistic personality disorder. Afterward, you will read about some treatment options and management techniques you can try in order to try and save the relationship and help make your partner a more stable, empathetic individual.

In the third part, you will learn about some warning signs that the state of your relationship with your narcissistic partner is too toxic or dangerous and you should leave without trying to salvage it. After reading these warning signs, you will read about how to effectively and safely get out of a toxic relationship with a narcissist.

How to Identify a Narcissist

In the broadest sense of the term, a narcissist is a person who is only concerned with his or own selfish wants and needs. When he or she does show any concern for the needs and wants of another person; it is primarily to gain the attention or admiration of that person. That is, a narcissist is not genuinely interested in any other person's wellbeing or happiness. Feigning interest in another person's needs or wants is one of the ways in which a narcissist manipulates others.

Due to a variety of different factors, a narcissist acts manipulative, self absorbed, and will often oscillate between extremes of depression and grandiose beliefs. This is because, at their root, they suffer from a severe lack of self esteem and, instead of dealing healthily with that low self esteem, project it onto others and try to regain a sense of self worth by acting as if he or she is the most important individual in the world.

However, there is not just one type of narcissist. Researchers have identified at least five subtypes based upon the specific behaviors and techniques by which a narcissist regains a sense of self worth. Those subtypes are as follows:

The Unprincipled Narcissist

The unprincipled narcissist shows the most difficulty in expressing empathy or showing intimacy. They share many personality attributes with individuals suffering from antisocial personality disorder (also known as sociopaths which you will read more about in the next chapter). Millon, a famous psychologist, identified the unprincipled narcissist as one who lacks a conscience and acts extremely deceptively or exploits others for his or her own gain.

This type of narcissist will lie without showing any regard for the consequences of those lies or how they might affect others. The unprincipled narcissist typically has a very dominating personality and is usually very stubborn or unable to make even the slightest compromises in any situation. This makes them very difficult to be in a relationship with as they will often use emotional abuse in order to get their way without having to compromise.

They have a weak sense of morality and have little ability or motivation to distinguish between what is right and wrong. This can make them extremely dangerous people when they are not undergoing any sort of treatment to manage the disorder.

The Amorous Narcissist

The amorous narcissist is a very charming type. They expend a lot of effort to be sexually seductive and appealing to others. They are often very clever, witty and have a way with words. This is where the primary dangerous lies as they often resort to lying and manipulation in order to create this charming persona which easily attracts many others.

Despite their charm, however, the amorous narcissist is entirely unable to build a truly intimate relationship. They do not express their true feelings and have no regard for the feelings of the other person in the relationship. If they are in a committed relationship, they will often have multiple affairs without any concern for the consequences. They also lack any respect for personal boundaries and will break apart other relationships without any remorse (such as by seducing and sleeping with married or otherwise unavailable people).

Because they are so manipulative and seductive, they can cause a lot of emotional pain to others and manipulate them into doing things they otherwise would never do. Once they have gained the attention, admiration, or love of another person; the amorous narcissist often loses interest and will abandon the individual leaving that individual heartbroken and regretting any actions he or she might have done while under the influence of the amorous narcissist's manipulative techniques.

The Compensatory Narcissist

The compensatory narcissist is different from the other subtypes in a very important way. While all narcissists suffer from a deeply rooted lack of self-esteem or sense of inferiority, the compensatory narcissist struggles with this in a more noticeable way. The use of narcissistic behaviors in order to overcompensate for those feelings is much more obvious. Therefore, the dramatic mood swings which all narcissists experience are much more pronounced in the compensatory narcissist.

This type of narcissist is under the impression that if others can be convinced of the narcissist's high self worth and value, it will get rid of his or her own feelings of inferiority. This, of course, never works because self esteem is something which must be built up from within and cannot truly be gained from any external source.

For this reason, the compensatory narcissist is often passive aggressive and shares some characteristics with avoidant personality disorder (like hypersensitivity, trust issues, and a dependency on fantasy or imagination in order to escape from the destructive low sense of self esteem). That is, the compensatory narcissist is passive aggressive because he or she is dependent upon the approval of others in order to feel a temporary sense of self worth but resents that dependency and resents his or her own inability to have a real sense of self esteem.

This type of narcissist is not as dangerous as the other subtypes at first. However, they still rely on many techniques of emotional abuse in order to manipulate those around him or her. This often causes a great deal of pain especially during the times when the compensatory narcissist becomes avoidant and distances him or herself emotionally from others.

The Elitist Narcissist

The elitist narcissist (often also known as the phallic narcissist) has an exaggerated view of his or her own power, influence, or privilege. He or she feels as if the entire world is owed to him. This type often feels an inflated sense of entitlement and demands special status in most situations regardless of whether or not such special status is deserved. He or she will also often demand favors or reward for accomplishments he or she may or may not have truly accomplished. The elitist narcissist feels that their social position is extremely high and that he or she is superior to all others.

This type of narcissist is very closely related to the generalized or nonspecific type of narcissistic personality disorder. The elitist narcissist shows extremely high levels of pride even while he or she has few actual accomplishments on which to base this pride. This is because he or she has no motivation to actually earn that pride or make him or herself deserving of that which he or she feels entitled to. Instead, the elitist narcissist uses manipulation and other emotionally abusive techniques in order to get whatever it is he or she feels entitled to have.

It is this that makes the elitist narcissist so toxic in a relationship. He or she will feel as if the partner owes everything to him or her without having to give anything back in return. This leads to a heavily one sided relationship in which the partner grows exhausted and begins to feel defeated while the elitist narcissist feels an inflated sense of power and entitlement.

The Fanatic Narcissist

Similar to the compensatory narcissist, the fanatic narcissist struggles with his or her low sense of self worth in a much more visible way. The difference lies in the causes behind it. While a compensatory simply lacks any self esteem and, instead, tries to gain that self esteem from others; the fanatic narcissist holds him or herself up to unrealistically high standards that are impossible to meet. When he or she inevitably falls short of those standards, the levels of self esteem plummet. In order to regain that sense of self worth, then, the fanatic narcissist seeks it out in others.

Thus, the fanatic narcissist is enduring a constant struggle between his or her own suppressed self esteem and his deep rooted need to achieve not mere success but complete perfection. Both the lack of self esteem and the unrealistic personal standards are illusory, however, and neither reflects the true value of the individual. However, because he or she is unable to realize the illusory nature of these two conflicting beliefs, the fanatic narcissist will often express similar characteristics as people with paranoid personality disorder (characteristics such as delusional thoughts, paranoia, and disorganized thoughts).

Sometimes they compensate for their low self esteem through fantasies or delusions of their own heroism and superiority. At other times, they will be trapped in a deep depression in which their low sense of self worth leads them to the delusional belief that they will never amount to anything at all since they cannot achieve the impossible high standards they have set for themselves.

The fanatic narcissist is less a danger to others than they are to themselves. This constant battle between two conflicting perceptions of themselves makes them highly unstable and even suicidal. Furthermore, the paranoia which they often suffer from makes it very difficult for treatment to be effective. Although this type of narcissist is less prone to using emotional abuse to manipulate others into fueling their need for self esteem; that does not mean they do not do it at all.

The primary issues you may encounter in a relationship with this type of narcissist, however, are going to be lack of trust, severe mood swings, and paranoid or delusional beliefs about you or the relationship.

Causes of Narcissistic Personality Disorder

Unfortunately, narcissistic personality disorder is still not fully understood. Researchers are still looking into the precise causes, symptoms, and treatment methods for the disorder. With that said, there are many contributing factors which are thought to potentially result in an individual developing narcissistic personality disorder. In 2006, the following list of potential causes was put together by Leonard Groopman and Arnold Cooper:

- Hypersensitivity: from birth onward, some people are simply more sensitive than others. That is, they react more strongly to criticism or punishment than others. Therefore, those with hypersensitivity might have had an otherwise normal childhood but simply lacked the ability to deal with criticism or failure in a healthy way. This leads to the need to overcompensate or create exaggerated personal standards in order to overcome those feelings of inferiority which he or she developed throughout his or her life.

- Excessive praise from a young age: it is definitely important to praise children when they exhibit good or desirable behavior. Praise encourages children to continue these good behaviors. However, excessive praise or giving praise when it is undeserved can quickly lead to a heightened sense of self importance. The recent spike in narcissistic personality disorder in young adults today can, in part, be attributed to the popular movement of the 1990s and early 2000s which sought to praise children highly and make every single child feel special or exceptional. Undeserved praise or praise that is not in proportion to the actual behavior will lead the child to grow feeling entitled to excessive reward for comparatively little effort.

- Excessive discipline from a young age: even though excessive praise can lead to the development narcissistic personality disorder; opting for the alternate extreme of excessive discipline will not prevent that. In fact, it is just as likely to cause the disorder as excessive praise. This is because the lack of praise creates an exaggeratedly low self esteem which the child finds other, unhealthy ways to compensate for (such as manipulating others into believing in the superiority of the narcissistic individual). Parents who discipline their children excessively or give out punishments that are not in proportion with the bad behavior will instill a deep rooted sense of inferiority that the child will struggle with late into his or her adult life. Individuals with compensatory or fanatic narcissism are far more likely to have experienced excessive discipline or criticism in childhood than those with other types of narcissistic personality disorder.

- Overindulgence of desires or impulses in childhood: in other words, giving a child anything he or she wants can result in the development of narcissistic personality disorder. It will instill in the child a sense that he or she is entitled to anything he or she wants without having to earn it. There is good reason this overindulgence is referred to as "spoiling" your children.

- Extreme emotional abuse in childhood: those who were emotionally abused as a child are far more likely to be emotionally abusive toward others when they grow up. Unfortunately, there is comparatively little being done in society to prevent emotional abuse (relative to physical abuse). However, emotional abuse in childhood can lead to a large number of dangerous or unhealthy personality disorders later in life (such as narcissistic personality disorder) which will make the individual incapable of achieving real happiness or satisfaction in life.

- Unreliable or inconsistent care giving throughout childhood: children who grew up with unreliable parents or bounced around from foster home to foster home never get that feeling of security or safety that comes with having one stable home life. This feeling of security is necessary for a child to develop into a healthy and confident (but not arrogant or narcissistic) adult. The instability also denies them the early childhood practice in forming strong emotional bonds with others.

- Having a narcissistic parent: although narcissistic personality disorder is not exactly hereditary, a narcissistic parent will often make some key mistakes in parenting that will result in their own child developing narcissistic personality disorder. The parent will often give either excessive praise or excessive criticism (or alternate between the two, confusing the child's sense of how to value right and wrong). They will often also be emotionally abusive. Furthermore, children learn a lot simply from watching their parents so the child of a narcissistic parent will learn to behave in narcissistic ways.

- Certain brain abnormalities: some research has started to suggest that actual brain abnormalities may exist in the brains of those with narcissistic personality disorder. There is a specific region of the brain (known as the left anterior insula) which is responsible for regulating our emotional responses and allowing us to feeling empathy or compassion. In the brains of narcissistic individuals, this region is underdeveloped or deficient. Whether this is caused by brain injury, a hereditary disorder, or simply develops from the other environmental factors that cause narcissistic personality disorder is still unknown.

Whatever the root causes of narcissistic personality disorder may be, it is deeply seeded in a strong sense of shame or inferiority. These are feelings the narcissistic individual would never admit to having. This is partly because they are ashamed of the very feelings themselves and partly because they are not fully aware of the feelings themselves having repressed them so deeply into the subconscious.

Therefore, at this subconscious level, every single narcissist feels irreparably inferior or defective. He or she believes that everything they are is completely unacceptable or unfitting in conventional society. They are incapable of knowing their real strengths and weaknesses. This is why they react so poorly to any sort of criticism or disagreement and will often become completely frustrated or unmotivated in the face of even the slightest setback. This makes it extremely difficult for them to follow through on many of their long term goals as the slightest opposition or obstacle will deter them completely.

It is important, then, to understand those behaviors which are associated with narcissistic personality disorder as defense mechanisms which the individual uses to cope with those deeply rooted feeling of shame or inferiority. When helping your partner deal with his or her disorder, you should make sure to keep this in mind in order to make sure that you remain sensitive to those subconscious feelings rather than the superficial (and often faked) consciously expressed feelings.

Treatment and Management Techniques You Should Try

Over the past few decades, a variety of different treatment and management techniques for narcissistic personality disorder have been developed. It is worth noting, however, that none of them are guaranteed to work in every single case and many must be used in combination with other techniques in order to see any real results.

How effective treatment will be for your partner will depend primarily on how willing he or she is to cooperate throughout the process of treatment.

In a perfect world, your partner will be willing from the beginning to go to therapy. If your partner is willing to take treatment seriously, long term, out-patient therapy is an extremely effective method for treating narcissistic personality disorder. In some cases the therapy will be combined with medication in order to help minimize some of the more severe symptoms of the disorder.

However, there are no specific medications approved by the FDA for the treatment of narcissistic personality disorder. Despite this, many people have benefited from the use of other medications designed to treat other disorders. For example, antidepressants have been shown to help reduce those underlying feelings of inferiority or shame. In addition, antipsychotics can help reduce paranoid or delusional thinking. Finally, psychiatrists will often use mood stabilizers in order to minimize the unpredictable and dramatic fluctuations in moods.

When out-patient therapy and medication are not enough, hospitalization may become necessary. Because your partner will probably refuse to acknowledge this necessity on his or her own; it is your responsibility to stay aware and keep an eye out for the key signs that hospitalization is the necessary next step. It is widely accepted in the medical community that hospitalization is required when any one of the following criteria are met:

a) Your partner is a threat to his or her own personal safety
b) Your partner is a threat to the safety of you or anyone else
c) Your partner is no longer capable of taking care of his or her most basic needs without assistance.

In case hospitalization may become necessary, it is important not to approach it as a punishment or consequence for your partner's inability to recover on his or her own. Instead, treat this personality disorder as you would any other illness and express sympathy. However, do not allow your sympathy to be exploited.

Hospitalization can be extremely beneficial to your partner. He or she will likely realize just how serious the problem has become and might realize how important it is to participate in his or her own treatment and take it seriously. Furthermore, while in the hospital, your partner will receive intensive care that can go a long way toward making your partner more receptive or responsive to out-patient treatment once he or she has been released. In almost every case, the hospital staff will determine a course of treatment to be continued after release from the hospital. This may include individual therapy, group therapy, medication, or some combination of these different options.

While your partner is going through all of this, there are some things which you can do in order to support your partner in his or her treatment and improve the state of your relationship. Your support and ability to help manage the disorder at home will help make sure that the treatment your partner is receiving becomes more effective. With that in mind here are some tips for what you can do:

- Stay calm: remain calm and patient when dealing with your partner. He or she will become increasingly vulnerable as the treatment continues and even a slight loss of temper or impatience can affect your partner strongly at this point. Their psyche is undergoing a complete overhaul and is, therefore, very fragile. Be prepared for some relapses to old behaviors and remain strong. It gets worse before it gets better.

- Be a source of support: one of the likely causes of your partner's narcissism was a lack of real emotional support. Make sure that your partner can feel safe and secure with you and that you are always there for him or to confide in without fear of judgment.

- Stay vigilant: narcissists are, by definition, manipulative. So stay cautious and keep a look out for false signs of recovery. They may pretend to take the treatment seriously or pretend to get better just to manipulate you into staying with them. In order to help you recognize these signs, you may want to go to therapy with yourself and let your therapist offer guidance and advice throughout the process.

- Know when to leave: it is a sad truth that treatment does not always work. If your partner does not seem to be making any improvement even after attending therapy for awhile, you need to be strong and just leave. The problems will only get worse and you need to get out before you he or she hurts you severely.

Warning Signs it is Time to Leave

- Constant lying: if your partner is lying to you, there is no trust in the relationship. The biggest warning sign is when they lie about extremely important things such as having an affair.

- Angry outbursts: everyone loses their temper but narcissists can become enraged at the flip of a switch. In this outburst, they will often use abusive language and mock or demean you. If your partner regularly experiences these angry outbursts, you need to get out.

- Manipulation: people who love each other do not feel the need to manipulate each other. Period. If your partner does anything to manipulate you, the relationship is toxic and extremely unhealthy. You should never be forced by anyone to do something you are not comfortable doing.

- Fear: if you ever feel afraid of your partner, you should end the relationship immediately. Fear has no place in a healthy, loving relationship.

- Putting aside your own needs: relationships are give and take. And sometimes, you will put your needs second to your partners (such as when they are sick or going through an emotionally trying time). However, these are temporary moments and your partner should be just as willing to put his or her needs aside when you are experiencing one of these temporary problems. If you are constantly putting your own needs second to your partners and getting nothing in return, this is an unhealthy and unbalanced relationship.

How to Get Out Safely

The warning signs you just read are all symptoms of emotional abuse. One of the biggest issues with emotional abuse is that the victim often has difficulty recognizing their own abuse. However, if any of these signs sound familiar to you, that is emotional abuse and you need to leave. Here are some tips for getting through the process of leaving your narcissistic partner:

- See a therapist: start going to therapy regularly. Professional guidance and support can be invaluable in this difficult and trying time and can make sure you heal from the ordeal in a healthy way.

- Build your support network: your friends, family, and even therapist will all form an invaluable network of support as you go through this. Keep them close and don't be afraid to depend on them while you are in this vulnerable emotional position. They know you would do the same for them in similar circumstances.

- Cut off contact: your ex partner will try to make contact with you. Do not allow it. It will be easier to recover and resist his or her manipulative techniques if you do not have any contact with him (or as little contact as possible).

- Get rid of reminders: just like cutting contact, getting rid of all those little reminders will help to make the break up feel real and make it clear that he or she really is out of your life.

- Put yourself first: pick up old hobbies or find new hobbies. Do things that you have always wanted to do but never had the chance while in that toxic relationship.

This will help you build a new life independent of your partner and show you that happiness and fulfillment is possible outside of that toxic relationship.

- Remember to grieve: you are going to feel depressed, angry, miserable, lonely, and a number of other things before you finally start to feel better about the decision you have made. Find a safe space to grieve (whether it's a person you confide in or a creative outlet you can express yourself with). Going through the grieving process now will ensure that you heal fully and healthily.

Chapter 2: Abusive Relationships with Sociopaths

As mentioned earlier, a sociopath is someone who suffers from antisocial personality disorder (or, dissocial disorder). The term "sociopath" has been used in popular culture to refer to anyone who has frequent trouble with the law or is generally difficult to get along with. However, these people are not necessarily sociopaths. If you are concerned your partner may be a sociopath, read the following section on how to identify a sociopath.

How to Identify a Sociopath

The attributes and behaviors used to diagnose antisocial personality disorder in an individual include:

- Inability to comply with social norms
- Lack of respect for the law
- Deceptive behavior such as lying, using fake names, or conning others

- Engaging in the behaviors listed above purely for personal pleasure or profit
- Impulsive; not planning ahead
- Irritability and/or aggressiveness
- Frequently gets into altercations or physical fights with others
- Reckless; lack of regard for safety (own safety or that of others)
- Chronic irresponsibility; unable to hold down a job or meet obligations
- Lack of remorse; indifferent toward or rationalizing mistreating or causing pain to others

These behaviors should be consistent in the person. Depending on how long you have known him or her, you should ask friends and family members that have known your partner for many years in order to ask if these behaviors have been ongoing or only recently started.

If they have only begun recently, they are likely symptomatic of some other problem. If possible, consult a professional psychiatrist or psychologist in any case as such behavior is dangerous whether it is part of antisocial personality disorder or some other issue.

The causes of this disorder can be linked to both genetic/physical and environmental factors. The genetic and physical factors include:

- Hormones: certain traumatic events occurring in earlier stages of development (puberty and prior) can disrupt the normal development of a person's central nervous system. The central nervous system is responsible for regulating the release of hormones. When development of this system is disrupted, the overall development of the individual is disrupted.

  For example, testosterone is one of the hormones that can be thrown off balance when the central nervous system fails to develop normally. Testosterone plays an important role in impulsivity and aggressiveness. Individuals with antisocial personality disorder tend to have significantly higher levels of testosterone.

- Neurotransmitters: there are important neurotransmitters in our brain which work to regulate and stabilize our moods. Studies have shown that people with antisocial personality disorder have drastically lower levels of the neurotransmitter serotonin. When serotonin levels are too low, the person has little control over his or her mood and can fluctuate between extreme highs and lows. Low serotonin levels have also been linked to irritability and aggressive behavior.

The environmental factors which can contribute to the development of antisocial personality disorder include:

- Parents with antisocial personality disorder: while the disorder is not strictly genetic; children are heavily influenced by their parents and tend to adopt many of the same behaviors that they saw growing up. Therefore, if one or both of the parents exhibits the behaviors of a sociopath, the child will likely grow up to be a sociopath as well.

- Head injuries: injuries to the head are one environmental cause which can lead to the problems discussed above. This is exactly the sort of traumatic event which—if occurring at the right time—could disrupt the central nervous system and throw the balance of the hormones off.

- Lack of strong bonds in early childhood: some studies of foster children have shown that when children are deprived of strong emotional bonds with others during these formative childhood years, they fail to develop the ability to form such bonds later in life.

- Irregular or inappropriate discipline: when authority figures are inconsistent or too excessive in their punishments, this could cause the child to grow up without the ability to distinguish right from wrong or appropriately judge the consequences of his or her behavior.

- Child abuse: studies have shown that people with antisocial personality disorder are more likely to have been abused as children than those with other disorders. This is particularly the case for early child abuse such as shaking an infant. Too vigorous of shaking can cause brain injuries which disrupt the normal development of the central nervous system.

Regardless of the causes, sociopaths can be dangerous, particularly to those who are closest to them. They have a high tendency to become emotionally abusive to friends, family members, and even their partners.

A sociopath is manipulative, disloyal, and lacks empathy. He or she becomes easily agitated and may even become aggressive. This can be extremely dangerous.

Treatment and Management Techniques You Should Try

Unfortunately, antisocial personality disorder is one of the most difficult personality disorders to treat. This is primarily because sociopaths are characteristically resistant to treatment. They lack the motivation to take treatment seriously and, in most cases, fail to realize that they may need treatment in the first place.

Further exacerbating the issue is the fact that sociopaths are so manipulative. They may go through the motions and pretend to become more empathetic by simulating remorse. However, as soon as the treatment is over, they will resume their old destructive behaviors.

However, they are not entirely unresponsive and a skilled psychiatrist or therapist can make real progress with a sociopath. In order for treatment to be most effective, the sociopath should be required to participate by some external source (such as the authorities or a personal relation). Residential or in patient programs are particularly effective because they provide a rigid schedule and carefully structured environment along with close supervision.

An intensive form of therapy known as multi systemic therapy has also been shown to be effective. This form of therapy requires the full cooperation of family members and the romantic partner.

The most effective individual therapeutic approach seems to be foregoing any attempt to instill a sense of conscience in the sociopath. Rather, a therapist is better off using rational or utilitarian arguments in order to motivate the sociopath to avoid destructive behaviors.

As a partner, you can attempt such a strategy yourself. Tell your partner that certain troublesome behaviors should be stopped not because they are immoral but because they could have negative consequences. For example, if your partner becomes easily agitated, tell him or her to practice calming methods and relaxation techniques in order to avoid future troubles with authorities or missing out on opportunities.

If your partner has difficulties holding down a job, encourage him or her by explaining that the paycheck is a worthwhile reward rather than attempting to explain the value of being responsible and reliable.

Medications may also be helpful in some cases. While there are no specific medications approved by the FDA to treat antisocial personality disorder, psychiatrists have been able to successfully treat some of the more dangerous symptoms. Antipsychotic medications are helpful in treating the aggressive behaviors while antidepressants or mood stabilizers have been helpful in regulating moods.

Using these medications in conjunction with therapy can make therapy more effective. This is because in alleviating these most severe symptoms, the sociopath will be more relaxed, stable, and open to cooperating with the treatment.

In managing your life with a sociopath (assuming he is getting treatment and hasn't yet shown any of the warning signs which will be discussed in the next section) there are a few things you should and should not do. Let's begin with the things you should not do:

- Do not make accusations: because sociopaths are easily agitated, making accusations is particularly risky. If you are trying to bring up an important problem, phrase it in a calm, reasoned manner that doesn't sound like an accusation. For example, instead of saying "I hate it when you insult me," try saying "I would appreciate it if you tried to avoid using these words." Alternatively, try to use only positive statements. For examples, instead of accusing your partner of insulting you, ask him or her to make more of an effort to compliment you.

- Avoid becoming emotional: sociopaths have difficulty with empathy and are easily distressed by signs of negative emotion toward them. This does not mean you should bottle up your feelings and try to ignore them. Instead, try to remain outwardly calm and express yourself in a rational and reasoned way. Instead of saying triggering phrases like "I hate," "I'm angry," or "I'm upset," try explaining that this problem is not acceptable and will not contribute toward a functional relationship. For example, say your partner lies about small things such as taking out the trash when he or she hasn't done so. In this case, don't become emotional or visibly angry. Instead, explain how lying and letting the trash build up will cause problems like insect infestations or unpleasant smells.

- Do not make ultimatums: ultimatums are, at their root, a form of manipulation and a seasoned manipulator does not take kindly to a taste of his or her own medicine. As they say, you can't fight fire with fire. If you want to help a sociopath develop healthy behaviors, you need to make the extra effort to set a good example. Do not use manipulative techniques or play games. Instead, show your partner how a healthy person deals with their problems.

- Do not use "right" or "wrong": this is similar to not making accusations. A sociopath lacks a fundamental understanding of right and wrong and will interpret your attempt to tell him or her that a certain behavior is wrong as an accusation. Instead, talk about "beneficial" or "not beneficial"; "helpful" or "unhelpful."

Now that you know what things to avoid doing, here are some things that you should do when working with your sociopathic partner to salvage the relationship and create a better future:

- Do engage in conversation: sociopaths need mental stimulation almost constantly. Think of all the topics you agree on or enjoy talking about and talk about them frequently. The more pleasant conversations you have with each other, the easier it will be for your partner to develop a real emotional bond with you as he or she goes through treatment and becomes capable of doing so.

- Do be supportive: remember to compliment every good behavior or positive trait you see in your partner. As you read earlier, one of the potential causes of antisocial personality disorder is excessive punishment and irregular discipline in childhood. Providing positive reinforcement wherever possible will help reverse the damaging effects of the childhood experience.

- Do change the subject: if you see that your partner is clearly trying to provoke or upset you, do not take the bait. Change the subject to something less volatile. This will help you avoid becoming upset or angry and it will help your partner realize that he or she does not have the power to control your emotions. Both of these are important in managing life with a sociopath.

- Do see a therapist: while your partner is in therapy, it is a good idea for you to be in therapy as well. Therapists are a great source of strength and support. They can also help guide you through the difficult and often overwhelming process of helping your sociopathic partner recover.

For more information on how to treat and manage someone with antisocial personality disorder, you should consult a professional counselor or psychiatrist, preferably one who specializes in this disorder. Do some research about what sort of support groups and other resources are available to you and your partner. Above all, do not be afraid to ask for help. This is a difficult situation and no one should do it alone.

Warning Signs it is Time to Leave

While there are some circumstances in which you can still manage to salvage the relationship with a sociopathic partner; there are some points at which you simply have to pack up and leave. Some people are so toxic that the risk of trying to stay and help them is too great. The best thing you can do in these cases is simply walk away. Here are some warning signs that it is time for you're to go:

- Physical abuse: at the very first instance (no matter how small you might think it is) that your partner's aggression becomes physical, you need to leave. Being physically abused is dangerous not only to your psyche but to your physical health as well. There is absolutely no excuse to abuse a person you love. So if your partner felt real love toward you, he or she would not even be capable of abuse. Do not let any excuse or rationalization convince you otherwise.

- Threatening violence: if your partner is using threats of violence in order to control you, this is an early warning sign of physical abuse. Getting out now can save you a lot of pain and suffering in the future.

- Feelings of depression: if you have felt noticeably depressed, lethargic, or numb lately; these are signs that you are being emotionally abused. Emotional abuse is just as severe as physical abuse and you cannot allow yourself to be a victim of it. Depression may not seem like a serious warning sign at first but it can lead to isolation and even suicide.

- Feelings of anxiety: if you feel anxious or nervous without any direct cause (or the direct cause is your partner), this is another sign of emotional abuse. This is unacceptable. Chronic anxiety is detrimental to your health and wellbeing. In extreme cases, it can cause heart problems and weight gain.

- Fear for your safety: if you ever fear for your life while with your partner, this is an absolute red flag that you need to get out. Your partner should make you feel safe and secure. You should never feel threatened or worry that you might be abandoned at any moment.

- Becoming isolated: when your partner keeps you from seeing friends and family, this is a sign of emotional abuse and an attempt to control you. It is dangerous to be so isolated from your social circle when you are living with a sociopath. Even if he or she is getting treatment, you should still be in close contact with your social circle so that you have a source of support outside of your partner. So if he or she is getting treatment but still isolating you from others, you need to get out now.

How to Get Out Safely

If you notice even one of these warning signs in your relationship, you need to get out as soon as possible. This can be extremely difficult but it is possible. The techniques for getting out of a toxic relationship with a sociopath are similar to those of getting out of one with a narcissist. In case you skipped that chapter, here they are again:

- See a therapist: start going to therapy regularly. Professional guidance and support can be invaluable in this difficult and trying time and can make sure you heal from the ordeal in a healthy way.

- Build your support network: your friends, family, and even therapist will all form an invaluable network of support as you go through this. Keep them close and don't be afraid to depend on them while you are in this vulnerable emotional position. They know you would do the same for them in similar circumstances.

- Cut off contact: your ex partner will try to make contact with you. Do not allow it. It will be easier to recover and resist his or her manipulative techniques if you do not have any contact with him (or as little contact as possible).

- Get rid of reminders: just like cutting contact, getting rid of all those little reminders will help to make the break up feel real and make it clear that he or she really is out of your life.

- Put yourself first: pick up old hobbies or find new hobbies. Do things that you have always wanted to do but never had the chance while in that toxic relationship. This will help you build a new life independent of your partner and show you that happiness and fulfillment is possible outside of that toxic relationship.

- Remember to grieve: you are going to feel depressed, angry, miserable, lonely, and a number of other things before you finally start to feel better about the decision you have made. Find a safe space to grieve (whether it's a person you confide in or a creative outlet you can express yourself with). Going through the grieving process now will ensure that you heal fully and healthily.

Chapter 3: Abusive Relationships with Psychopaths

As mentioned in the introduction, psychopaths are very similar to sociopaths. In fact, the psychiatric community still argues about how one should accurately distinguish between them.

Generally speaking, the emotional abuse you face in a relationship with a psychopath is going to be the same as that which you experience with a sociopath. So if you are concerned that your partner may be a psychopath, read the previous chapter about sociopaths to learn how to effectively deal with your situation.

Bearing that in mind, there are some key distinctions between the two terms and the type of people that they identify. First of all, the term "psychopath" is more often used within the justice system and criminology while "sociopath" is more widely accepted within the medical community.

Because of this difference in usage of the terms, a psychopath is far more likely to be a criminal or have a criminal background. While it is also very common for a sociopath to have experienced trouble with the law in the past, a psychopath is essentially guaranteed to have a criminal record.

A psychopath is also much more prone to physical abuse than a sociopath (who relies more on emotional abuse). Psychopaths are prone to violent outbursts and even sexual assault, making them a particularly dangerous type to live with.

Like a sociopath, psychopaths have difficulty with empathy, morality, and recognizing the pain they are causing others. Unlike a sociopath, however, a psychopath is much more likely to suffer from a learning disorder of some kind. This means that they are not the charming, smooth talkers that sociopaths or narcissists so often are. In fact, some studies have shown that psychopaths often have a lower than average IQ.

The causes of psychopathology are complex and varied. They also differ in many important ways from the causes of antisocial personality disorder. The roots of psychopathology can be found in both genetic and environmental causes.

Genetic causes are primarily attributed to something called the Warrior Gene: every human being has a gene called monoamine oxidase A (MAO-A). This gene is also known as the "warrior gene." It is responsible for helping the body break down and process neurotransmitters such as serotonin and dopamine. Both of these neurotransmitters are key players in regulating our mood and making us feel good.

In a certain variation of the monoamine oxidase A gene, the body produces less of the MAO-A enzyme. Studies have shown that levels of MAO-A activity are linked with higher aggression and even psychopathology. This is because the lower levels of activity means that less serotonin and dopamine are being processed in the brain.

Without those neurotransmitters, a person becomes prone to aggressive or violent behavior and exhibits significantly less control over his or moods.

Environmental factors are very similar to that of people with antisocial personality disorder. Psychopaths tend to have a history of child abuse, traumatic head injuries, or poor parenting.

The most important thing to note is that psychopaths are generally much more dangerous than narcissists, sociopaths, and any other type of toxic person. Not only do they lack empathy and morality, they are more prone to violence and sexual assault. This makes them a threat of both emotional abuse and physical abuse.

Because of this, there are essentially no circumstances in which you should stay and try to salvage a relationship with a psychopath. If you find that you are in a relationship with one, get out immediately.

Use the advice found in the other chapters of this book to create a plan for eliminating this toxic psychopath from your life and moving on. Reach out to trusted family members and friends for additional support. If possible, join a support group or start seeing a therapist.

Chapter 4: Abusive Relationships with Toxic People

In this chapter, you will gain a broader sense of how to deal with toxic people in general. While each of the above three types can be classified as "toxic," there are many, many more people that can be a toxic influence in your life. In those cases, you need to know how to identify this toxicity in general.

How to Identify a Toxic Person

As healthy people have different traits embedded in their personality, so do the people with problems. The only difference between the healthy person and a person with mental problems is the balance of these traits which is well maintained in the healthy person and one can guess how it is in a person with mental/psychological problems. For example, we all have narcissistic trait in us but what makes a narcissist, a narcissist is imbalance in his narcissistic traits.

One can have this imbalance in more than one trait for example narcissism and dependence. It might sound ridiculous when one reads that a person can have an imbalance in narcissistic and dependent traits at the same time as it makes us believe that the person is narcissist and dependent at the same time which is not the point here. The point is that the same person could be very narcissistic regarding some specific things but at the same time very dependent regarding the others.

Imagine a grown man who is very good at business which is his work, goes to office and looks down at all his colleagues which obviously creates problems for him and for others working in the office. The same person goes home in the evening and realizes that his wife is not at home and starts to panic and that is because he does not know how to function at home in his wife's absence. His wife comes home after sometime and he starts to scream at her. Could we call him narcissist and dependent? Technically yes, as the psychological diagnostic manuals have a provision for diagnosing the person with more than one psychological disorder and even multiple psychological disorders. Such a person with an imbalance in more than one psychological trait in laymen's term is labeled as a toxic person.

Which means that a sociopath can also be psychopath; narcissist can also be a sociopath and so on. The degree of difficulty building/having relationships with such people is usually much higher. Toxic people are also very well known for "polluting" people around them. Like in the example above, the person creates problems for his colleagues and his wife and might also end up leaving psychological scars which could be difficult for them to get out of. It is usually very difficult to identify such people as the traits in which they show the imbalance differ from each other and sometimes are even opposite to each other. In order to identify a toxic person, their behaviors, actions and thoughts have to be looked at in different settings. Another way of identifying such people is to be more aware of one's self and to notice how such people makes one feel.

For example, every parent tries to be a little strict with their kids in order to teach them boundaries. In most of the cases it leads to some unpleasant feelings on the child's part. If these parents are strict only when the child does/wants to do something wrong, the child learns what is wrong. Imagine parents who scold the child for everything he/she does, what impact would that have on the child? The child will not only be confused between the right and wrong but most importantly will be polluted by the by his/her parents aggression and will feel unpleasant all the time especially around his/her parents.

Let's do a little exercise in order to learn how identify toxic people. Look back in your past and think of an incident where you made a mistake and were scolded by somebody that bad that it made you feel terrible. Later on you realized that you did make a mistake but you did not deserve that kind of scolding. Because the person scolded you in order to make sure that you don't repeat the same mistake again; you still thought that the scolding was an exaggeration and that you could have got the point without an extreme scolding. If you can think, remember such a situation, you have already met a toxic person. In this case you being aware of what you need in order not repeat mistakes could help you to point out an exaggerated reaction from a toxic person. It is very important to differentiate the unpleasant feeling arising from within as a reaction to a situation and the internalized unpleasant feeling of another person in order to identify a toxic person.

In case you are still unsure, take the simple quiz below to help figure out whether or not you are in a toxic relationship:

1. When it comes to your partner or the relationship in general, you feel like you can't do anything right.
   a. Yes
   b. No
   c. Not sure/I don't know

2. It is starting to seem more and more as if everything is about your partner and little respect is given for your own feelings or opinions.
   a. Yes
   b. No
   c. Not sure/I don't know

3. The good moments in the relationship are starting to become fewer and farther between.
   a. Yes
   b. No
   c. Not sure/I don't know

4. You find yourself walking on eggshells or unable to really be yourself and speak your mind when with your partner.
   a. Yes
   b. No
   c. Not sure/I don't know

5. Your relationship with your partner has become a source of judgment or struggle rather than support and encouragement.
   a. Yes
   b. No
   c. Not sure/I don't know

6. Your partner has used threats of force (or even actual physical force) to make you do something you otherwise would not do (or not do something you otherwise would do).
   a. Often
   b. Never
   c. Once or twice, perhaps

7. Your partner uses disrespectful language, excessive criticisms or degrading language with you.
    a. Often
    b. Never
    c. Once or twice, perhaps

8. You feel afraid of your partner.
    a. Often
    b. Never
    c. Once or twice, perhaps

9. Your partner threatens to abandon or alienate you in order to manipulate you into doing something you otherwise would not do (or not doing something you otherwise would do).
    a. Often
    b. Never
    c. Once or twice, perhaps

10. Your partner makes most of the decisions in the relationship (and even most of the decisions in your own life).

   a. Yes

   b. No

   c. Not sure/I don't know

11. You feel as if you are growing more and more apart from friends and family that you were once very close to.

   a. Yes

   b. No

   c. Not sure/I don't know

12. Your partner has lied to you about something which you consider to be important (and which your partner knows you consider to be important).

   a. Often

   b. Never

   c. Once or twice, perhaps

13. You have witnessed your partner lying to others (especially if he or she lied about something that you consider to be important).

    a. Often

    b. Never

    c. Once or twice, perhaps

14. Your partner blames you or places a lot of guilt on you for any problem affecting the relationship or any concerns you might bring up.

    a. Often

    b. Never

    c. Once or twice, perhaps

15. Your partner experiences dramatic mood swings. Sometimes he or she is ecstatically happy, other times he or she is impossible to be around; and your own mood is determined entirely by the mood of your partner.

    a. Yes

b. No

c. Not sure/I don't know

16. You feel that you put much more effort into caring for your partner's needs than your partner puts into caring for your needs.

   a. Often

   b. Never

   c. Once or twice, perhaps

17. If your partner has done or said something wrong, he or she will not admit to it or take responsibility for it.

   a. Often

   b. Never

   c. Once or twice, perhaps

Now tally up your answers and determine which of the four categories below most reflect your results:

Mostly A's

If you answered mostly A's in this quiz, there is a very high chance that your relationship is not only toxic but your partner is suffering from one of the personality disorders discussed in the previous chapters. Many of the statements in the quiz are signs of emotional abuse so if you are experiencing this many of them, you are likely being emotionally abused. Seek out a trusted friend or family member to provide you with guidance and emotional support as you work through this situation (either by getting your partner into therapy or leaving the relationship altogether).

Mostly B's

If you answered mostly B's, this is good news. Your partner is probably not toxic and you don't need to worry about severe emotional abuse. With that said, certain toxic habits can form in otherwise normal relationships. So if you chose A for any of the statements in the quiz, you need to make sure to address those issues with your partner and resolve them before they grow into one huge, insurmountable divide between the two of you.

Mostly C's

If you have answered mostly C's, this means you are still somewhat unsure about whether or not your relationship is toxic or you are suffering from emotional abuse. You need to take the time to examine your relationship and your partner more closely. If you feel as if you are in a fog or unable to clearly see the state of your relationship, reach out to a trusted friend or family member and ask their opinion and advice. When your partner is emotionally abusive, it can become extremely difficult to identify that clearly. This is a direct side effect of emotional abuse in you. Don't feel bad for being unable to recognize whether or not you are being emotionally abused. Instead, reach out for help in figuring it out.

Equal amount of A's and B's

If you have an equal (or near equal) amount of A's and B's in your responses, this can mean one of two things. It may mean that you are in an otherwise healthy relationship that simply has some serious issues to work out. In this case, an honest, open discussion of the issues with your partner should help to begin the process of resolution. If that seems too difficult, seeking out a couple's counselor or therapist may help open up the lines of communication and get things back on track.

The second option is that you are, indeed, in a toxic relationship. If this is the case, the fact that you still have a lot of B's in your responses could indicate that the emotionally abusive behavior is still not so severe that it is irresolvable. Therapy for both you and your partner (individual therapy as well as couple's therapy) may help rebuild a strong, healthy relationship.

However, you must be cautious, even if you responded to only half of the statements with A's, this is a sign that there are undoubtedly toxic elements in your relationship. It may, in fact, be the case that you are in a toxic relationship with an individual who suffers from a severe personality disorder and you are simply too influenced by the emotional abuse to see this clearly. This is why it is always important to seek out the opinions of others whom you can trust.

Treatment and Management Techniques You Should Try

There are various different ways of dealing with such people which are listed below:

1. Confrontation: A very effective but risky technique of confrontation is often used to make toxic people realize their toxicity. It is very important that these people are confronted in a very smooth way and are served with proper grounds for them to realize the malfunctioning in their behavior. Expression of genuine feelings towards their offensive and harsh statements could be one of those smooth methods. Confrontation might not

necessarily change their behavior but might motivate them to seek for further help. If not done right, confrontation might lead to toxic people becoming more toxic and aggressive.

2. Seeking psychotherapy: Psychotherapy could be of great help to such people only if they could be made to realize that they have a problem and they need to seek help. It is also recommended for people who are related to such people to visit a psychotherapist as it might help to distinguish their own problems from the toxicity of the toxic people. There are some schools of psychotherapy which could be more helpful in this specific problem. Psychoanalysis, one of the first and very popular methods could be useful in helping the person to understand the patterns behind the toxic behavior. Systemic therapy could help the person to see himself as a part of the system and

how his behavior influences the people in the system and hence lead to a motivation to change. Cognitive behavioral therapy could also be very helpful to fix the problem much faster by practicing certain exercises on therapists' recommendations. Certain kind of group therapy could also help the person to come out of his own perspective and look at his problem from the perspective of other people.

3. Meditation and Yoga: Yoga and Meditation are very old but very efficient methods of becoming more self-aware. They could help calming down the toxic person if needed and could prove to be very useful in self reflection.

Warning signs it is time to leave

If you come across the following situations, it might be time for you to start questioning your relationship with the toxic person:

1. Rigidity to acceptance: Acceptance is usually the first step in the direction of a change. If the toxic person you are in a relationship with is very rigid to accept or to even reflect on his disturbing behavior (towards others or you), it could become very difficult to do anything about the person and your relationship with the person.

2. Rigidity to change: One might come across people who are very self-aware or let's say seem to portray themselves as very reflective. Some of these people even being aware of their problem show rigidity towards change. It might because they are afraid of losing themselves or their identities. According to Sigmund Freud, the father of psychoanalysis, these people have a very week ego structure. It is usually very difficult to help these people as they don't give much value to other people opinions about themselves

and might keep living in a bubble of their own.

3. Crossing boundaries: If the pollution level exceeds a certain point, it might be very important for the person in a relationship with the toxic person to protect himself/herself. Repeated verbal and physical abuse and accusations might be a clear sign for this person to keep the toxic person away from his or her surroundings. If staying away is not a possibility (and it's the case of repeated verbal abuse), one should at least keep oneself mentally strong when encountering this toxic person.

How to Get Out Safely

If you happen to realize that the toxic person you are related to or are in relationship with isn't ready to accept his or her problem; isn't ready to change; or you have had enough of him or her, you should think about getting out of the relationship with this person. When that time comes, it will be very important to do this very carefully as you wouldn't want this to disturb your own psychic balance and have an influence on your future relationships. As mentioned in the beginning of the chapter, toxic people could have an imbalance in different psychological traits.

So, it might be sensible to figure out those psychological traits and deal with them accordingly. For example, if it is a partner of yours who has a very dependent personality, you might want to end the relationship slowly and softly as it could traumatize your partner and he or she could end up taking some extreme steps like following you around and may be even threatening or trying to kill him or herself.

For this reason, make sure you have somewhere safe to go such as a friend or family member place. Let the person you are staying with provide you with the support you need right now to get through this. If your former partner calls or otherwise attempts to contact you, have this person talk to him or her instead of allowing him or her to see or speak with you. The emotionally abusive techniques your partner has used to manipulate you will not work on your friend or family member.

It is also a good idea to keep a journal of all the emotionally abusive behaviors your former partner has and how they have affected you. This way, you have a constant reference of all the toxic elements that caused you to leave the relationship. More importantly, it will help you to see clearly the pain and damage that was caused in that relationship and make you better able to resist any further emotional abuse by being able to recognize it from the beginning.

Conclusion

The purpose of this book is to help guide you through the difficult process of recognizing and eliminating the toxic people in your life, no matter what form they come in.

The information provided in the previous chapters has focused on dealing with toxic romantic relationships. However, it can also be applied to other relationships such as friends, family members, coworkers, and anyone else who may be emotionally abusive.

Suffering from emotional abuse can cause you to feel overwhelmed, lost, or hopeless. Hopefully, by reading this guide, you have reached some sense of clarity and feel surer about the next steps you need to take in order to create a life for yourself that is healthy, fulfilling, and enjoyable.

Getting out of a toxic relationship is the first step toward making room in your life for people who will give you the emotional support and love that you need and deserve.

Always stay cautious of the warnings signs you have read about in this book and remember that you deserve happiness. Be strong and take charge of your life. True happiness in life is possible.

Keep this book on hand for reference as you work through the difficult process of effectively eliminating the toxic person or people in your life. The next step is to reach out to trusted friends and family for additional support. You should also do some research about what resources (such as therapists or support groups) are available in your area.

Thank you for reading and good luck on your journey!

20499381R00051

Printed in Great Britain
by Amazon